TOP SECRET SCIENCE IN TRANSPORTATION

Megan Kopp

CRABTREE
PUBLISHING COMPANY
WWW.CRABTREEBOOKS.COM

TOP SECRET SCIENCE

Author: Megan Kopp
Editors: Sarah Eason, Honor Head, Claudia Martin, and Ellen Rodger
Proofreaders: Sally Scrivener, Tracey Kelly, and Wendy Scavuzzo
Editorial director: Kathy Middleton
Design: Lynne Lennon
Cover design: Paul Myerscough and Jeni Child
Photo research: Rachel Blount
Production coordinator and prepress technician: Ken Wright
Print coordinator: Katherine Berti
Consultant: David Hawksett

Produced for Crabtree Publishing by Calcium Creative

Photo Credits:

t=Top, tr=Top Right, tl=Top Left

Inside: NASA: pp. 3, 26–27t; Nikola Motor Company: pp. 8–9t; NURO: p. 19r; Shutterstock: Sergei Afanasev: p. 6; Asharkyu: p. 37; Ceri Breeze: p. 42; Grzegorz Czapski: pp. 1, 44; FedBul: p. 36; Sheila Fitzgerald: p. 15r; Hadrian: p. 24; Iurii: p. 7; Anna Kireieva: p. 31b; Kletr: pp. 10–11t; Ivan Kurmyshov: p. 13; Frederic Legrand – COMEO: p. 33r; James R. Martin: p. 11t; Metamorworks: pp. 5b, 25; Petrmalinak: p. 40; PP77LSK: p. 16; R.nagy: p. 38; Ruigsantos: p. 12; John Selway: p. 27c; Steve52: p. 21; Sundry Photography: p. 20; Mino Surkala: p. 17; Suwin: pp. 4–5t; Temp-64GTX: pp. 18–19t; U3d: p. 45; Yauhen_D: pp. 22–23b; YMZK-Photo: p. 39; University of Michigan: pp. 22–23t; Virgin Hyperloop One: p. 41; Volocopter: p. 43; Wikimedia Commons: Jeff Foust: pp. 30–31t; Gpski: p. 29; Hellbus: p 34; S Kaiser: p. 28; Library of Congress: pp. 14–15t; Alexander Migl: pp. 32–33t; N509FZ: p. 35; Ubahnverleih: pp. 8–9b.

Cover: Shutterstock: Andrey I.

Library and Archives Canada Cataloguing in Publication

Kopp, Megan, author
Top secret science in transportation / Megan Kopp.

(Top secret science)
Includes index.
Issued in print and electronic formats.
ISBN 978-0-7787-5997-3 (hardcover).--
ISBN 978-0-7787-6035-1 (softcover).--
ISBN 978-1-4271-2246-9 (HTML)

1. Transportation--Research--Juvenile literature. 2. Transportation--Technological innovations--Juvenile literature. I. Title.

HE192.5.K67 2019 j388 C2018-905666-5
C2018-905667-3

Library of Congress Cataloging-in-Publication Data

Names: Kopp, Megan, author.
Title: Top secret science in transportation / Megan Kopp.
Description: New York, New York : Crabtree Publishing, [2019] | Series: Top secret science | Audience: Ages 10-14. | Audience: Grades 7 to 8. | Includes index.
Identifiers: LCCN 2018053421 (print) | LCCN 2018058564 (ebook) | ISBN 9781427122469 (Electronic) | ISBN 9780778759973 (hardcover : alk. paper) | ISBN 9780778760351 (pbk. : alk. paper)
Subjects: LCSH: Transportation engineering--Juvenile literature. | Transportation--Juvenile literature. | Trade secrets--United States--Juvenile literature. | Technological innovations--United States--Juvenile literature. | CYAC: Transportation engineering. | Transportation. | Trade secrets. | Technological innovations.
Classification: LCC TA1149 (ebook) | LCC TA1149 .K66 2019 (print) | DDC 629.04/6--dc23
LC record available at https://lccn.loc.gov/2018053421

Crabtree Publishing Company
www.crabtreebooks.com 1-800-387-7650

Printed in the U.S.A./042019/CG20190215

Published in Canada
Crabtree Publishing
616 Welland Ave.
St. Catharines, ON
L2M 5V6

Published in the United States
Crabtree Publishing
PMB 59051
350 Fifth Avenue, 59th Floor
New York, NY 10118

Published in the United Kingdom
Crabtree Publishing
Maritime House
Basin Road North, Hove
BN41 1WR

Published in Australia
Crabtree Publishing
Unit 3 – 5 Currumbin Court
Capalaba
QLD 4157

CONTENTS

RL 201
25201

CHAPTER 1

ON THE MOVE

Transportation is all the methods of moving quickly and safely from one place to another, by land, water, and air. But what really goes on behind the scenes? What deals are made and secrets stolen to make it to the top of the transportation industries? Cutting-edge technology can make huge **profits**. The transportation industry is very competitive and the money that can be made encourages companies to be ruthless in keeping their science and technology a secret from competitors who might steal it to make money from it themselves.

Transportation is changing. Today, cars, trains, ships, and planes are not just faster than ever before, but smarter, too.

AUTOMOBILE SECRETS

The global automobile manufacturing industry is worth a staggering $2 billion. Such huge sums of money bring out the secret and sometimes dark side of business—and of some businesspeople. Car companies are very secretive when developing new technology, especially technology connected to self-driving vehicles.

STEALING SECRETS

A former Apple engineer has been accused of stealing **trade secrets** related to Apple's self-driving car project. Trade secrets are closely guarded devices or techniques used by a company in making its products. They are the **intellectual property** of the company. Intellectual property is ideas that are protected by law so that no one else can use them without the owner's permission. Information was **allegedly** downloaded to the employee's personal computer a few weeks before he quit to join a self-driving startup in China. He was arrested and the legal case is ongoing.

TOMORROW'S SECRETS

Imagine a day when vehicles talk to each other. It is coming. Vehicle-to-vehicle (V2V) communication allows vehicles to **wirelessly** exchange information about their speed, location, and direction. Vehicles, not the humans behind the wheel, become aware of other vehicles in the area. Your car might use the messages it receives from other vehicles to decide if there is a potential crash threat. It can send this information to the driver with an alert, such as a sound or a visual sign on the car dash. Alternatively, it can take immediate action, such as turning the steering wheel or applying the brakes.

One day, pedestrians and bicycles may be able to use V2V communication to allow motor vehicles to see them even when the driver cannot. This could help save many lives.

BENEATH THE SURFACE

Sleek and deadly black, submarines glide through the dark depths of the oceans, killer machines ready to strike at a moment's notice. Famous inventor Leonardo da Vinci had an idea for an underwater vessel in the 1500s, but he kept his sketches a secret because he was worried about their misuse. Secretive by their very nature, the development of submarines has always been powered by the latest—and most closely guarded—science.

GOING NUCLEAR

Like nearly all transportation, most ships depend on **fossil fuels**, such as oil, coal, and natural gas, to run motors. Burning fossil fuels creates pollution, and the planet does not have an unlimited supply of these fuels. Refueling also requires making regular stops, which is something that stealthy military submarines prefer not to do. The use of **nuclear power** for ships was originally a top-secret suggestion considered by the U.S. government in the 1940s. By 1989, there were more than 400 nuclear-powered submarines globally.

A nuclear reactor produces energy by splitting the nuclei of atoms, the tiny particles that are the building blocks for everything

Russia keeps the designs of its submarines top secret, but gave the world a glimpse of its Vladikavkaz sub, codenamed Paltus, during a 2018 parade.

on Earth. A risk of nuclear reactors is that, if they accidentally release that energy, particularly in a small, hard-to-escape space such as a submarine, it is deadly. In 1961, this happened onboard the Soviet submarine *K-19*, killing 22 crewmen.

SECRET SUBS

The U.S. navy's designs for new nuclear submarines are a closely guarded secret. At present, navy designers are at work on a faster, more powerful submarine, the *Columbia*-class. The cost of designing the vessels, without even building one, is estimated at $4.2 billion. The *Columbia*-class will have propellers turned by super-quiet electric motors, making them stealthier than other subs.

Currently, all U.S. navy submarines are nuclear powered.

DARK SCIENCE SECRETS

In 2015, the United States and China agreed to a **truce**, banning private companies from using the Internet to steal trade secrets. Three years after signing the truce, Chinese **hackers** got into the computers of a company working for the U.S. navy. Information about submarine and undersea weapons technology was stolen. This means that China now knows what weapons are carried by U.S. submarines, and at what distance U.S. submarines can detect enemy submarines. This will give the Chinese an advantage in the event of any hostilities between China and the United States.

PROTECTING SECRETS

Companies need to protect their new money-making inventions from being copied by others. Patents are licenses that give owners the sole right to make and profit from their inventions for a set period of time. Patents are important because they prevent original ideas from being used by someone else while an invention is being perfected, which can take a long time.

PROBLEMS WITH PATENTS

A problem with patents is that they often contain technical information about an invention, so once a patent is approved by the U.S. Patent and Trademark Office (USPTO) it becomes public knowledge. New inventions can be worth billions of dollars because companies need new technology to stay ahead of their rivals. Sometimes, companies decide that keeping the details of an invention secret is a better choice, so they decide not to patent their invention.

Nikola claimed the **aerodynamic** shape of their **semi-truck** was a unique design feature and sued Tesla for $2 billion.

TESLA TROUBLES

In 2018, the automaker Tesla was sued by a **hydrogen** truck company, Nikola Motors. Hydrogen-powered vehicles are a new technology that uses the energy in hydrogen atoms. The hydrogen energy is usually released by a **chemical reaction** between hydrogen and oxygen in a fuel cell. A fuel cell changes that energy into electrical energy. Nikola Motors claimed Tesla copied their patents and that Tesla's all-electric semi-truck has similarities to their own hydrogen-electric semi-truck. These include such things as the aerodynamic body. Curved shapes and transportation trucks do not mix, as they are designed to maximize space, making them boxy. An aerodynamic truck faces less **air resistance**, which means it needs less fuel to travel at the same speed.

DARK SCIENCE SECRETS

In 2016, pictures of one weird bus went **viral**. China's Transit Elevated Bus (TEB) was extra-wide and ran on tall "legs," rather like a moving bridge, so it straddled traffic. The city of Beijing built special tracks for the giant, electric-powered vehicle. However, there were immediate doubts that the bus was strong enough to hold the weight of passengers. In 2017, a **prototype** bus stalled mid-track. Police investigated and arrested 32 of the people behind TEB on suspicion of **fraud,** because they had made false claims about the bus to get people to invest their money. The prototype now rusts in storage.

The TEB, shown here as a model, stood 16 feet (5 m) tall and was 26 feet (8 m) wide.

CHAPTER 2

THE ROAD AHEAD

Today's automotive industry is very competitive. Ideas are carefully guarded, while design laboratories and test tracks for new models are kept hidden from spies with prying eyes. Performance tests are run years before a new vehicle model hits the showrooms. To test a new part, companies will put the part in another vehicle already in production. This second vehicle, called a mule, is used to disguise the new part so no one knows it is being tested.

CAMERA SPIES

Need to hide something? Then fire off a smoke bomb! That is what some automakers are doing to hide test track vehicles from spy **drones**. To study the performance of a new vehicle, automakers have to do thousands of test miles. This testing is done years before the vehicle goes on sale, but automakers want the design to be new and exciting when it is officially revealed.

Spy photographers are always watching big car companies for opportunities to take photographs of new cars being tested. They can sell these photographs for a lot of money. Drones are often used to spy on test cars. Some automakers have drone detectors on test tracks to alert them if a drone is nearby. If there is a drone, they let off a smoke bomb or pull the cars off the track, then hide them inside tents.

Rival automakers and journalists eager to get a story use drones to spy on new car models.

The **camouflage** on the rear of this prototype car is intended to keep the bumper design a secret.

INVISIBLE CARS

General Motors, Ford, and Fiat Chrysler are often called the Big 3. These large automakers have headquarters in Detroit, Michigan, and keep high-speed racetracks and other testing areas nearby. These facilities are closely guarded and the perfect starting place for testing new vehicles. However, eventually, manufacturers need to test in slow-moving city traffic, while still keeping their inventions secret. This is where car camouflage comes in. Most manufacturers use a black-and-white pattern, making it difficult for the eyes to focus on the car's shape because it blends in with its surroundings. The vehicle travels in full view, but the details of its shape are hard to see.

DARK SCIENCE SECRETS

Electric car maker Faraday Future claims that a former employee took trade secrets about its **artificial intelligence (AI)** technology for his new company, EVelozcity. AI is cutting-edge programming that lets computers make decisions by following complex rules. When perfected, AI will enable cars to react to road conditions in a split second. In 2018, Faraday Future began a lawsuit against EVelozcity. The company denies that it has broken laws.

DIRTY SECRETS

Climate change is making Earth's temperature rise and causing more extreme weather events, such as hurricanes and floods. A major cause of climate change is burning fossil fuels, which releases carbon dioxide, a greenhouse gas. Over the past few years, journalists and campaigners have uncovered company reports that reveal that some oil companies and car manufacturers have known about the link between gasoline and diesel engines and climate change for decades. Fearing for their profits, these companies kept their knowledge secret and continued doing things as they always have. This is one of the industry's dirtiest secrets.

CHEATING THE TEST

In 2018, *The New York Times* revealed that the oil industry is looking for cracks in the system to make car **emissions** standards less strict. The paper claimed that the oil industry even paid for ads on Facebook that urged people to write to the government to lower emission standards. Emissions tests check for carbon dioxide, as well as carbon monoxide, which is **toxic**. They also test for hydrocarbons, which can cause **smog**. If a car releases too much pollution, it must be fixed before the vehicle is allowed to run on public roads. In the United States, the Environmental Protection Agency (EPA) sets the levels that car manufacturers must meet. In Canada, Transport Canada and other government agencies set standards. Some companies will go to great lengths to beat the emissions tests.

Different countries have different levels of emissions control. In the United States, California leads the way with stricter standards than those set by the federal government.

DARK SCIENCE SECRETS

In 2015, the German car company Volkswagen admitted that it rigged millions of diesel engines to lower its ratings on emissions tests. More than 10.5 million vehicles were affected. The company was known for its low emissions. However, cars sold in the United States had software in the engines that could tell when they were being tested. The computer turned on systems that lowered emissions, then shut them off again when not being tested. This gave the testers a false record of how much pollution was being sent into the air. Nine former Volkswagen senior executives were criminally charged in the United States, and two were sentenced to prison terms. The company paid $1.2 billion in fines.

Today, Volkswagen cars, such as this Passat Alltrack, are not rigged to cheat emissions tests.

ELECTRIC SECRETS

Electric cars are nothing new. The first electric car was introduced more than 100 years ago and remained popular in U.S. cities until the mid-1930s. But there were problems. Electric cars cost a lot to build and could travel only a short distance before needing to recharge. Gasoline-powered vehicles were cheaper to mass-produce on the new assembly lines of the early 1900s. The electric car idea faded away and gasoline-powered engines became the norm. Then, in the 1970s, there was a gasoline shortage. When the secret of climate change became common knowledge, manufacturers started looking at electric car technology again.

HIDING THE TRUTH

To move away from fossil fuels, car manufacturers and energy companies have to create new technology and **infrastructure**, including electricity charging stations instead of gas stations. Although it is keeping quiet about it, the industry built from fossil fuels is not in a hurry to make changes. Electrifying the automobile industry would be catastrophic for the profits of many companies. For the time being, most automakers are focusing their efforts on **hybrid** vehicles, which have both an electric motor and a gasoline or diesel engine. In this way, most automakers are dipping their toes in the electric market by creating just one or two hybrid models. The exceptions are new companies that specialize in electric cars, such as Tesla. Tesla is leading the way both with its cars and its charging stations. Could the latest automaker secret be that the big car companies are waiting for Tesla to perfect the technology and create the charging stations before taking the electric plunge themselves?

Gasoline-powered cars were first mass-produced by Ford Motor Company in the early 1900s. Will Tesla do the same in the future with electric cars?

SABOTAGE!

In 2006, Tesla started producing an all-electric sports car that could travel more than 200 miles (320 km) on a single **battery** charge. Tesla is at the top of the growing electric car market, but it is facing strong competition from other forward-thinking companies. The company also claims it was **sabotaged** by a former employee. In 2018, Tesla accused a former employee of hacking into its computers and sending data, including confidential photos, to several people outside of the company. The employee claimed he was simply drawing attention to issues with Tesla's batteries.

TOMORROW'S SECRETS

A fully electric vehicle gets its energy for driving from energy stored in its battery. It must be plugged into an electricity outlet to recharge. Recharging electric vehicles is currently slow. It takes the same amount of time to charge a Tesla as it does to fill the tanks of 80 gas-powered vehicles. Some battery manufacturers are looking to switch to **supercapacitors**. While batteries store energy in chemicals, capacitors store it as an electric charge.

There are more than 1,300 Tesla charging stations, such as this one, around the world. It takes 75 minutes for a Tesla car to charge.

BATTERY WARS

Batteries are the life of electric cars. The goal is to go faster and farther with electric power. The race is on to be the first to create the best electric car battery. The winner will corner the market and make huge profits, so it is no surprise the latest technology is kept top secret. Currently, China is the biggest producer of electric car batteries, followed by Japan and South Korea. Many American universities are researching new battery technology.

Currently, the batteries in an electric car are relatively large, heavy, and expensive.

DANGER!

Many electric cars use **lithium-ion batteries**, but they cannot hold a very large electric charge. This means that a vehicle running on these batteries can travel only about 200 miles (320 km) before it needs charging. This is fine for city travel, but not for long-distance trips.

There is another burning issue with lithium-ion batteries. They can burst into flames if the vehicle carrying them is involved in an accident. The fluid inside the batteries is highly flammable so the resulting fire is extremely hot and difficult to put out. Burning lithium-ion batteries also produces a mixture of harmful gases, including carbon monoxide. Until lithium-ion battery technology improves, any increases in production of all-electric cars could also mean increases in dangerous vehicle fires.

This Nissan Leaf car is part of a fleet of electric taxis in the city of Amsterdam, in the Netherlands.

RACE TO THE FINISH

Given the dangers of lithium-ion batteries, solid-state batteries may be an alternative option that will take electric vehicles farther. Solid-state batteries replace the liquid inside lithium-ion batteries with a solid material, such as ceramic or glass. These small-but-mighty batteries are becoming the focus of car manufacturers around the world. Toyota, Nissan, and Honda are joining forces to work on solid-state batteries in Japan. China's CATL and BYD battery makers are in the race for the next technological advance. Samsung and Hyundai are firing up the technology in Korea. Germany's Volkswagen AG is working with QuantumScape Corporation. And many American startup companies are also now beginning to challenge the bigger car manufacturers in the race to create the perfect electric car battery.

14:30 PM

TOMORROW'S SECRETS

The need for electric cars is spurring on many new inventions in the world of batteries. One new solution could be uBeam technology, the brainchild of then-25-year-old science graduate Meredith Perry. It uses **ultrasound**, or sound waves that cannot be heard by humans, to transmit electricity. Power is turned into sound waves, sent through the air, then converted back to power upon reaching the electrical device. This opens up the possibility of cars never having to stop to recharge at all!

CHAPTER 3

SELF-DRIVING CARS

Self-driving cars do not have human drivers—instead, they have computers as their brains, cameras as their eyes, and Light Detection And Ranging (lidar) as the senses that help them understand what is happening all around. The better these technologies work, the safer the car—and the more money made. It is no wonder that these technologies are kept top secret!

Most autonomous cars send out pulses of light, called lidar, which bounce off surrounding objects.

LIDAR

One of the most important technologies in any self-driving car is lidar. Lidar sends out beams of light, not usually visible to humans, which bounce off surrounding objects and back to a **sensor**. Since light travels at a constant speed, the time taken for the beam to return tells the sensor how far away an object is. A lidar system creates a **three-dimensional (3-D)** map of the surroundings. The map is so detailed that it does not just see objects, it recognizes them. While most automakers believe lidar is essential, it is very expensive. Tesla's chief executive officer (CEO), Elon Musk, does not think it is necessary. Tesla is banking on his belief that **radar** (which works like lidar but uses radio waves instead of light), ultrasound, and powerful computer programs can do everything that lidar can do.

COLD, HARD ROAD

Self-driving cars are often tested in parts of California and Arizona where the weather is warm. But how do these vehicles cope with snow, ice, and fog? Falling snow and fog can affect the performance of technologies such as lidar. In the Aurora Project, VTT Technical Research Centre of Finland is testing **autonomous** cars in the Arctic Circle, where temperatures are constantly low. There, cars speed along on frozen surfaces and deal with snowstorms. Sensors have been installed in the test road to provide feedback for the engineers about how the vehicle is managing.

In 2018, Nuro launched the first unmanned grocery delivery service (see below).

TOMORROW'S SECRETS

Two former Google engineers have started a company called Nuro that builds self-driving vehicles—with a twist. They wanted to design a completely new kind of vehicle, overturning our ideas about what cars look like and what they do. The Nuro vehicles look like lunchboxes on wheels. The handle of the lunchbox is the self-driving sensors and cameras. The Nuro does not have seats inside because it does not carry people. Instead, there are compartments for groceries, drycleaning, or deliveries of online orders. When the car arrives, the customer punches in a code to pop open the side hatches and collect their goods.

EYE SPY

Uber and Waymo are just two of the companies trying to expand into the self-driving car market, because they know that this technology is the future of the business and where the big money lies. Both companies are testing similar technology in various locations in the United States. In 2017–2018, the rivalry between the two companies led to a trade secrets lawsuit.

PSST, DO NOT PASS IT ON

In 2016, a long-time engineer with Waymo left the company and joined Uber. It was alleged he took Waymo's lidar secrets with him and that Uber built autonomous vehicles using these trade secrets. On top of this, Uber's former manager of global **intelligence** testified that Uber had set up a new section in its company called Marketplace Analytics to steal trade secrets from its rivals. The manager claims Uber used a secret computer system so their spying would not be traced back to them. It automatically deleted messages after they were received. It is also claimed that former **Central Intelligence Agency (CIA)** agents were hired to help Uber with its spying. Less than a week into the trial in 2018, Uber agreed to pay Waymo approximately $245 million.

A Waymo self-driving car maneuvers in a parking lot, while a human driver sits behind the wheel.

In 2015, Uber started to develop self-driving cars, such as this one on a test drive in Pittsburgh.

DARK SCIENCE SECRETS

Those in favor of self-driving vehicles argue that removing human drivers from behind the wheel will actually increase safety, as human drivers can be distracted, careless, sick, or consume alcohol or illegal drugs. Others are not so sure that self-driving vehicles are safe enough—or, at least, not yet. In March 2018, a self-driving Uber vehicle killed a **pedestrian** in Tempe, Arizona. Uber temporarily stopped testing its autonomous vehicles in Phoenix, Pittsburgh, San Francisco, and Toronto. The death was believed to be the first pedestrian death connected to self-driving technology. A human tester was in the vehicle at the time, but she did not have time to react before the woman was hit. Two years earlier, a Tesla Sedan S failed to brake while using its autopilot (self-driving mode) technology. The car hit a tractor trailer, killing the car driver.

SECRET CITIES

Following the terrible Uber accident in Arizona, automakers were nervous about test-driving self-driving vehicles on public roads. So, some manufacturers came up with an idea—to build giant fake cities, complete with crossroads, roundabouts, traffic lights, and obstacles. In these fake cities, tomorrow's self-driving cars are learning how to drive without risking the lives of pedestrians and other drivers.

MADE IN MICHIGAN

The Mcity Test Facility was one of the first fake cities. Built by the University of Michigan, it is open only to testers and researchers. There are two-, three-, and four-lane test-track roads. Road surfaces vary from concrete and asphalt to brick and dirt. Each surface tests different reactions, such as how long it takes a car to stop, especially if it is raining.

A 1,000-foot (305-m) stretch of road is built to look like a freeway, with entrance and exit ramps, overhead signs, and guardrails. There is even a highway overpass that vehicles can drive under. The space below the overpass blocks wireless and satellite signals, to see if the car can still navigate when it cannot receive these signals.

Some automakers test their cars by placing robotic mannequins on test roads, to see if the cars avoid them.

Mcity, in Michigan, has fake two-story buildings, crossroads, and street signs, all built to learn what could confuse a car's sensors.

Car navigation systems, called sat nav, use the **Global Positioning System (GPS)**. GPS satellites send out radio waves, giving the time at which the signal left the satellite. These signals are received by sat navs. Since radio waves travel at a constant speed, the sat nav can calculate the distance to three or more satellites and figure out exactly where it is.

DRIVERLESS SHUTTLE

Based on the knowledge they have gained from years of testing at Mcity, researchers launched the Mcity Driverless Shuttle research project in June 2018. The shuttlebus picks up students and staff on a 1-mile (1.6-km) round-trip route. The study is looking at how passengers and people on the streets react to driverless shuttles—some people will not even get on a driverless bus!

DARK SCIENCE SECRETS

In self-driving cars, computers do all the work and are in control. One concern about self-driving technology is that hackers can take over computers, because their systems have connections to the outside world, such as wireless links for navigation. This means terrorists or criminals could take control of our cars and use them as weapons. In 2015, two hackers, Charlie Miller and Chris Valasek, hacked into—and drove—a Jeep Cherokee in order to demonstrate the risk. This led to the Jeep's manufacturer, Fiat Chrysler, withdrawing 1 million vehicles so they could improve security. Automakers, software developers, and security experts are working to prevent future hacking threats.

IT IS A SECRET

Back in 2014, rumors started to swirl that Apple—the tech giant behind the iPhone, iPad, and iPod—was working on an electric self-driving car, which everyone suspected might be called an iCar! The company never confirmed nor denied the rumors. Everyone was left wondering if Apple would launch its own car, or create an automated driving system for other car makers.

PROJECT TITAN

From the beginning, Apple was secretive about its plans, which were codenamed Project Titan. But tech experts and industry insiders started putting the pieces together. They speculated that the project was to build a self-driving electric car that would be released in 2023 or 2025. One of the first clues was when Apple hired a lot of engineers who had designed for other car companies, including Waymo, Tesla, Ford, and GM. Other new employees had been involved in producing electric vehicle batteries. Then, in 2017, Apple applied for a patent for a computer that can be used with self-driving systems. The company also received permission to test self-driving cars from the California Department of Motor Vehicles in April 2017.

Would an iCar have music, phone, and Internet connection all at the press of a button?

A few months later, Apple shared online that it would be running driverless shuttles to and from its head office. In December of the same year, the company's director of AI explained how far Apple had progressed with its self-driving technology. He revealed that the Apple AI system is capable of working in the rain and that it can identify where pedestrians are, even if they are hidden behind a parked car on the roadside.

Deep learning would take autonomous car technology to a whole new level. Cars could find their way across cities, changing routes to avoid traffic.

TOMORROW'S SECRETS

NVIDIA is a company that makes **computer chips**, which are tiny devices that hold all the "thinking" parts of a computer, including its memory. In 2018, the company revealed a new chip for use in self-driving cars, in partnership with Volkswagen. The chip will run NVIDIA's new AI programming. The AI teaches itself how to do tasks by watching a human do them first, adding to its own built-up experience. This advanced and complex type of AI is called deep learning. NVIDIA's technology will allow a car to decide when it is best to apply the brakes, which route to take, and at what speed to travel.

CHAPTER 4

UP, UP, AND AWAY

NASA is currently working on a single-pilot plane that will make only a soft "thump" when it passes the speed of sound.

The first successful airplane, built by the Wright brothers, took to the air in Kitty Hawk, North Carolina, in 1903. The plane flew for 12 seconds before it landed back on Earth. The Wright brothers had plenty of competitors for the title of first to fly, but their secret to success relied on repeatedly testing and improving on the design and materials used in their plane. Today, more than 100 years since the 1903 flight, testing has become industry standard.

SUPERSONIC

Dawn broke across California's Mojave Desert on October 14, 1947, to witness the most significant moment in aviation history since the Wright brothers' first flight. Charles E. Yeager, a former World War II (1939–1945) pilot, climbed into the U.S. Air Force's X-1 and took off. The Mach meter topped out at 1.02. Stronger, lighter, and faster, today's cutting-edge airplanes are **supersonic**, which means they travel faster than the speed of sound. Supersonic speeds are measured by Mach numbers instead of miles per hour. Mach 1 is the speed of sound, which is close to 770 miles per hour (1,240 kph). Yeager was the first person to travel faster than sound. The U.S. government did not stop its supersonic research there. Today, there are rumors it is developing a secret jet that will travel at Mach 6.

BOOM OR NO BOOM

Most supersonics are military aircraft. Only two supersonic passenger planes were ever built, the Concorde (1976–2003) and Tupolev Tu-144 (1977–1978), but both were retired because of problems with safety, cost—and noise. When something travels faster than sound, it creates shock waves in the air known as a sonic boom. This is a deafening noise that can even damage buildings. In 2018, the National Aeronautics and Space Administration (NASA) and Lockheed Martin announced they were working together to build a quieter supersonic plane. Eventually, the technology could be used for passenger planes, too.

Unlike the Concorde (right), supersonic planes of the future could fly quietly.

DARK SCIENCE SECRETS

The air transportation industry is, unfortunately, open to **cyberattacks**. In 2015, Polish airline LOT had to cancel and delay numerous flights after a successful cyberattack against their ground control system. Ground control organizes airplane movement on the ground, before and after flight. This could have led to a nasty accident if two planes collided. In 2016, Turkey's airport passport control systems were hacked. That same year, Vietnam's airport announcement systems were taken over. Whether cyberattackers are looking for secrets or trying to disrupt transportation systems, their actions risk lives.

STEALTH!

Airplanes need to be aerodynamic, which means they are shaped to maximize the forces that lift them off the ground, while minimizing air resistance. The extraordinary U.S. plane Tacit Blue, built in 1982, looked so un-aerodynamic that it was nicknamed "the Whale." Despite appearances, the Whale was a super-secret early stealth plane.

Tacit Blue had a maximum speed of 287 miles per hour (462 kph) and a length of 55 feet (17 m).

BOUNCING AROUND

Stealth technology allows vehicles to go almost unnoticed by radar, which means they can fly undetected in enemy territory. Radars send out radio waves, which bounce off objects and return to the scanner. This alerts the radar user to any vehicles in the area. However, stealth planes either absorb the radio waves, bounce them around, or offer very little surface for them to bounce off—or a combination of these methods. Back in the 1980s, when Tacit Blue was created, all this technology was still in development.

LEADING THE WAY

According to documents released by the CIA in 2013, Tacit Blue was tested at the U.S. government's Area 51, which is a top-secret military base in Nevada. It was a single-pilot plane, with an unusually wide cockpit. Tacit Blue's shape, full of flowing curves, like two curved whale tails, reflected radar waves. It was also built around a new type of system, Battlefield Surveillance Aircraft—Experimental (BSAX), which could bounce radio waves off in different directions instead of returning them to the scanner, making the system radar-proof. BSAX was large, which helps further explain the Whale's odd shape. While Tacit Blue never officially went into service, lessons learned from its development led to future stealth bomber designs such as the F-117A Nighthawk and B-2A Spirit.

DARK SCIENCE SECRETS

In 1957, Avro Canada rolled out the world's most advanced fighter aircraft, the CF-105 Avro Arrow. It was packed with weaponry and capable of flying at Mach 2, or 1,535 miles per hour (2,470 kph), for long periods of time thanks to its high-tech engines. In 1959, the Canadian government canceled the Arrow project and ordered all Arrow aircraft—as well as their models and designs—to be destroyed. In 2017 to 2018, nine models were found at the bottom of Lake Ontario, where they had been dumped. High costs and politics were given as the reasons for the canceling the Avro Arrow program, but the full story remains a mystery today.

Canada tried to sell the Avro Arrow to the United States, but it was worried about using foreign-made warplanes.

SOARING INTO SPACE

In the past, airlines concentrated on faster, safer, and cheaper ways to fly their passengers around the planet on vacation or for work trips. Today, some airlines are thinking bigger—way bigger. They are working on top-secret plans to fly their passengers into space for their vacations!

Tickets on SpaceShipTwo, seen here being carried beneath WhiteKnightTwo, will cost $250,000.

ABOVE AND BEYOND

In 2004, Richard Branson, owner of the airline Virgin Atlantic, announced his Virgin Galactic project, which would introduce space trips for the public. After 10 years of testing, one of his planes crashed, killing a pilot. Branson's dream rekindled in 2018, when pilots took off in a completely redesigned plane, the SpaceShipTwo VSS *Unity*. *Unity* is a two-pilot, six-passenger aircraft designed to take paying customers into space and back. It was launched from the air, released by a carrier plane called WhiteKnightTwo. The plane flew at Mach 2 before reentering the atmosphere and gliding down to a safe landing. A second flight took off two months later. Branson's team continues to work to cut down the time needed to refit the plane between flights from months to days. Branson hopes to be taking passengers to space soon, but he has competition. Amazon billionaire Jeff Bezos also has plans for space trips for the public. His rocket, *New Shepard*, which takes off vertically from the ground, is in the final stages of testing. It can travel at more than Mach 3. Which one will win this race for space?

TOMORROW'S SECRETS

Aircraft designers are always searching for new materials that will make their planes more lightweight, which will, in turn, make them fly faster and reduce fuel costs. Graphene could be one of those new materials. It is a form of carbon (which makes diamonds) that has its atoms arranged in a hexagonal pattern. It was developed in 2004 at the University of Manchester, England. It is super thin and light, yet super strong. In the future, it could be used to waterproof airplane wings. The aircraft manufacturer Boeing has developed a material called microlattice. It is made of hollow tubes that look like lace, making it light and **flexible**, or able to move easily. You could be sitting on it when you fly in the future!

The carbon atoms in graphene are arranged in a single layer and in an endlessly repeating hexagonal pattern. It is the strongest material ever tested.

FLYING CARS

In the late 1980s, Boeing spent $6 million to develop the Sky Commuter. It was the first of its kind—a complete prototype flying car. Three Sky Commuter prototype vehicles, with helicopter-like spinning blades, were built before the program was canceled for unknown reasons. It is thought that the idea did not have the technology to back it. There is no proof that the Sky Commuter had even one successful flight. Today, a number of companies are working on producing flying cars for the public.

AeroMobil has been in development since 1990, but its designers hope it will be on the roads–and in the air–within the next couple of years.

FOLDING WINGS

In Slovakia, a company called AeroMobil has developed a flying car, revealing its first prototype in 2014. The AeroMobil is capable of both driving on the road and flying in the air. Its 27-foot (8-m) wide wings fold out when the driver is ready to fly. In the air, it has a maximum speed of 124 miles per hour (200 kph), while on the road it can reach 99 miles per hour (160 kph). The company plans to have the first 500 vehicles on the market by 2020. A pilot's license and a driver's license will be needed by any driver. Terrafugia is another company designing cars with folding wings. Their TF-X is an all-electric flying car that will be able to unfold its wings and take off vertically, lifted into the sky by the rush of air from a fan.

ONWARD AND UPWARD

A Dutch flying car developer, PAL-V, has created a two-seat, gas-powered gyrocopter. Gyrocopters look like helicopters, as they both have horizontal spinning blades. However, in a gyrocopter, the blades are not powered by the engine—they turn only because of the air rushing through them. This spinning gives **lift**, which is the force that pushes an aircraft up into the air. Meanwhile, the driving power comes from a propeller at the back of the vehicle. Gyrocopters are suited to low-speed flight. PAL-V Liberty can fly at a height of 250 miles (400 km) and reach speeds of up to 100 miles per hour (160 kph).

TOMORROW'S SECRETS

Air travel is responsible for up to 9 percent of human-made greenhouse gases, which are contributing to climate change. Aircraft companies are looking at ways to improve the situation. A **solar-powered** plane called Solar Impulse 2 completed a stop-and-start flight around the world in 2016. Its body and wings were covered with more than 17,000 light-collecting cells, which turned the Sun's energy into electricity to power the plane. Each cell was roughly the thickness of a human hair. It took a year to complete the entire world trip, including all stops.

At 208 feet (63 m), Solar Impulse 2 had a wingspan larger than a big passenger plane, but weighed only as much as an average family car.

CHAPTER 5

TRAIN TECHNOLOGY

Trains have been around for more than 200 years, but breakthroughs have made them go faster and faster. The earliest trains were powered by burning coal to create high-pressure steam, which moved their wheels. They traveled at just 15 miles per hour (25 kph). Today's fastest train speeds along at 374 miles per hour (603 kph).

GOING GREEN

Many trains are powered by diesel fuel, which releases greenhouse gases when it is burned. Some rail operators are looking at ways to cut down greenhouse gas emissions by using less diesel. General Electric has built a hybrid diesel-electric locomotive, called the Evolution Locomotive. When a standard train brakes, it loses energy as heat, as the brakes press against the train's moving parts. Instead, the Evolution Locomotive reverses its motors to slow down the train. The unused energy is harnessed by the power system, thereby reducing diesel use.

GE's Evolution Locomotive saves energy lost during braking, so it can travel nearly 500 miles (800 km) on a single gallon (3.8 l) of fuel.

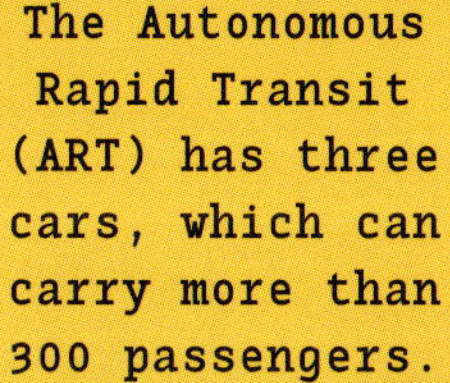

The Autonomous Rapid Transit (ART) has three cars, which can carry more than 300 passengers.

ALL ABOARD

A promising technology for replacing diesel entirely is to catch the energy from a vibrating, or shaking, railroad track. A train's movement creates a vibration in the track. A mechanical motion energy generator transforms this movement into power. Researchers in the United Kingdom and Switzerland are looking at a technique to allow electricity to flow directly from solar panels, which capture energy from the Sun, to electrified train tracks and trains themselves.

TOMORROW'S SECRETS

China is at the forefront of a transportation revolution that will combine buses with trains. The world's first trackless ART system is being tested on a 1.8-mile (3-km) route in central China. ART is an electric vehicle that is a blend of a bus and train. It runs on rubber tires and follows special white lines painted on the road instead of running on regular rail tracks. It is equipped with cutting-edge computer programs and sensors to help the driver follow the route and avoid obstacles. Because ART stays on the road, it costs one-fifth as much to run as similarly sized track trains.

KEEP ON ROLLING

Train technology is not the only aspect of rail transportation that is changing fast—the tracks are changing, too! Railroad tracks and bridges have to be checked carefully and maintained regularly to keep them strong and safe. Once-secret wartime technology can now help to spot damage that cannot be seen by the human eye.

Sound Navigation And Ranging (sonar) systems send out sound waves, then time how long it takes for the echo to return.

TRACKING THE TRACK

Companies that maintain tracks have self-driving cars that use cameras and sensors to "look" at the condition of the track, making sure the rails are perfectly straight and unbroken. Erosion, when soil and rock is carried away by rain or wind, around train bridge supports is often difficult to check, especially during floods. Railroads use sonar. Sonar, developed by the British Navy as a top-secret project during World War I (1914–1918), is a system that sends out sound waves to detect objects underwater. These waves bounce off the bridge supports and the ground surface below flood water. Based on the echo returned, engineers can tell if there is damage. Railroad companies also use ultrasound to see inside steel rails and check for damage. **Ground-penetrating radar**, which uses radio waves that can travel into the ground, builds pictures of the rocky bed of the track. Engineers study the results to look for hidden holes.

SENSING DAMAGE

Sensors placed along the side of the tracks examine the strength of trains' wheels as they pass. Bearings are small parts attached to wheels that allow them only to rotate, not wiggle out of line. As they prevent wobbles, **friction** can make them hot. Overheated bearings can cause a train to derail. Heat sensors, which take pictures of infrared, or heat, energy, check for signs of overheating.

TOMORROW'S SECRETS

Scientists in Europe are looking to change the way locomotives and railroad cars are built. A current study is investigating the use of 3-D printing and carbon fibers, which are extremely strong and lightweight threads. 3-D printing is a method of manufacture in which computers build objects using liquid materials, which then dry into a solid. Using this new and creative technique, they can create parts that are lighter than, and just as strong as, regular steel parts.

3-D printing technology has been in development since the 1980s, and can today be used to manufacture engine and train parts.

SECRET SPEED

When it comes to the world's fastest trains, the secrets of their technology are hard to find out—let alone understand. From magnetic trains to bullet trains, the competition is on to build faster trains, without putting passenger safety at risk.

MAGLEV TRAINS

The idea of a train that floats above the rails has been around for more than 100 years. Maglev trains, short for magnetic levitation, use **magnetic fields** to **levitate**, or lift, trains above the rails. Because there is no contact between the wheels and rails, there is less friction. Less friction means less wear, less maintenance, and better fuel consumption. Maglev trains do not have an engine. They work on the principle that the opposite poles of two magnets **repel**, or push away from, each other. A magnetic field is created in the train track, which pushes away the train, propelling it along the track.

The first high-speed maglev train was launched in Shanghai, China, in 2004. The Shanghai maglev runs from the airport to the city center. It travels at 268 miles per hour (430 kph).

The Shanghai maglev first hit the rails in 2004 as the fastest passenger-carrying railroad line in the world.

LO SERIES

Japan is working on a 9-trillion-yen ($111.4 billion), 320-mile (515-km) maglev line connecting the cities of Tokyo and Osaka. Most of the train will be underground, which will be costly and more difficult to build. The project is scheduled for completion by 2045. Its LO Series trains, which are currently being tested, are the fastest in the world, reaching 374 miles per hour (603 kph), although they will run at lower speeds when they are carrying passengers.

The "nose" of LO Series trains extends 49 feet (15 m) to improve its aerodynamic shape and reduce the noise of the train in tunnels.

DARK SCIENCE SECRETS

The problem with high speed is that mistakes can be deadly. Two high-speed trains collided in China in 2011, when one train stopped after a lightning strike. Almost 200 people were injured and 40 lives were lost. An investigation into the crash revealed attempts to cover up the causes of the accident. More than 50 officials of the railroad ministry were blamed for mistakes leading to the disaster, including ignoring the fact that control center equipment had flaws. After the accident, the top speed of the trains was capped at 186 miles per hour (300 kph). In 2017, some of the trains were once again allowed to run at 217 miles per hour (350 kph).

WHAT NEXT?

Which way will the world of transportation go next? Our vehicles are already faster, safer, smarter, and more environmentally friendly than in the past, so it is likely they will continue to travel in this direction. However, another development may be that the differences between train, car, ship, and plane, will continue to blur. With the latest top-secret technology, it is hard to tell what mode of transportation is being designed.

In the future, we could be traveling through giant tubes called hyperloops.

HYPERLOOP

In 2013, the technology billionaire Elon Musk proposed a new type of superfast, train-like transportation. He called it Hyperloop. Hyperloop "trains," which are more like wheel-less pods holding passengers, are propelled by maglev technology along an above-ground magnetic tube. To make them even faster, the tubes are nearly emptied of air, to reduce air resistance. The whole system will run on solar power. Elon Musk's company, SpaceX, has a short, 1-mile (1.6-km) test Hyperloop system.

PIPELINE PLANS

China's Aerospace Science and Industry Corporation is reportedly starting secret research into a hyperloop. Rumors suggest that top speeds would be close to 2,500 miles per hour (4,000 kph), which is faster than sound. One problem with such a fast train would be that passengers would feel unwell if the train accelerated (or sped up) too fast. To prevent this, the train will accelerate more slowly than passenger planes. Several other organizations are planning hyperloops, including TransPod, a Canadian company that aims to have a 620-mile (1,000-km) hyperloop operating between Canadian cities by 2030.

Richard Branson's company, Virgin, is developing Hyperloop One, which is being tested in the Arizona desert.

TOMORROW'S SECRETS

Sometime in the near future, visitors wanting to travel between Chicago's O'Hare International Airport and downtown Chicago will be able to do so in a speedy 12 minutes, thanks to another new piece of technology from Elon Musk's company. The route's existing transportation systems take between 35 and 50 minutes. A super-fast tunnel system will allow driverless battery-powered pods to whisk along a concrete track on electric-powered skates, at speeds of up to 150 miles per hour (240 kph).

UP IN THE AIR

As our roads become more overcrowded, many new forms of technology are taking off! They are taking to the air, or overhead tracks, so that they can avoid traffic jams at ground level.

POD CARS

The Personal Rapid Transit (PRT) is a new form of transportation for the future. It is made up of self-driving pod cars that ride on overhead guideways like tracks. Each small pod is perfectly sized for a family. The pods travel on demand. Passengers press a button to let the pod know where they want to go. There are more than six makers of this new technology around the world, each with its own variation. A few limited PRT systems are already in operation, including a 21-pod track at Heathrow Airport in the United Kingdom.

FLYING CABS

A flying cab service is a step up from drone delivery. Drones are pilotless

The PRT at Heathrow Airport connects the terminal with a parking lot. The pods are equipped with lidar sensors.

The Volocopter 2X is built from specially designed materials made of carbon fiber, which makes it extremely lightweight as well as strong.

airplanes that navigate using sensors and cameras. Some exciting new drones are large enough to act as cabs. Volocopter 2X is a helicopter that can be operated by a pilot or, where allowed, fly autonomously. This futuristic flyer is powered by nine high-capacity batteries. It is capable of carrying up to 352 pounds (160 kg) and has a range of 17 miles (27 km). There are plans to launch a cab service with the copter within the next five years. However, many hours of testing are ahead before drone companies can hope to get approval from the Federal Aviation Administration (FAA) for public use in the United States.

14:30 PM

TOMORROW'S SECRETS

Electric flying drones large enough to act as cabs may one day soon be everyday sights, as long as current testing keeps on going to plan. Volocopter will start running inner-city tests in Singapore in late 2019. The flight tests will fine-tune the cameras and sensors used to detect other airborne vehicles, buildings, and power lines. It will allow the company to assess the reliability of battery power. The tests will also provide the groundwork for the air-traffic control system that will be necessary to monitor a future city with thousands of flying cabs taking customers to their next destination. The testers will also consider how noisy a swarm of such drones might be!

BE A FUTURE TAXI DESIGNER

We have seen how science and technology are changing the way we travel. Imagine you own a transportation company. You have been asked to research and design a new form of self-driving cab. The look of futuristic transportation is in your hands.

YOUR MISSION

- Research what you would like your taxi to look like. Will it travel on the road, on some kind of track, or in the air? How will it be powered? Will it be environmentally friendly? What safety factors do you need to consider?
- Write a mission statement saying why you are building your taxi. Is it to make the roads safer or to save the environment? Explain what benefits your cab has for users.
- What already exists that could help you with your new design?
- What new tools or new technology would you have to develop to make your taxi a success?
- Would you be willing to share any new technology that you develop with other companies?

Do you think the future of transportation is in the air? What effect do you think that would have on your future?

TOP SECRET

How would you guard your design secrets, and what possible problems might be revealed by your testing? If something went terribly wrong, would you keep it a secret, or share your knowledge with the world?

GLOSSARY

Please note: Some **bold-faced** words are defined where they appear in the book.

aerodynamic Having a sleek shape that allows air or water to easily flow around

air resistance The force exerted by air on an object as it moves

allegedly Said to be true but not proven

artificial intelligence (AI) Computer programs that are able to perform tasks that normally require human brain power

autonomous Acting independently

battery A container that stores energy, ready to be converted into electricity and used as a source of power

camouflage Disguise that helps something blend into its surroundings

Central Intelligence Agency (CIA) A government agency that gathers and analyzes information concerning the security of the United States

chemical reaction A process in which two or more substances are changed into different substances

cyberattacks Attempts to break into and damage computer systems

diesel A liquid fuel heavier than gasoline

drones Pilotless aircraft

emissions Substances that are released, particularly pollutants coming out of a car's exhaust

fossil fuels Fuels such as coal, oil, and natural gas that were formed over millions of years from the remains of dead plants and animals

fraud Deceiving others to make money

friction The force that makes it difficult for one object to slide along the surface of another

greenhouse gas A gas that traps the Sun's heat in Earth's atmosphere

hackers People who break into computer systems using the Internet

hybrid A car that can be powered by both electricity and gasoline

hydrogen A colorless, odorless gas

infrastructure Systems and facilities of an area, such as roads and power lines

intelligence The collection of valuable information

lithium-ion batteries Batteries that store an electric charge by moving tiny electrically charged particles, or ions, through a liquid or gel

magnetic fields Areas around magnets or electric currents where the force of magnetism is felt

nuclear power Energy created by splitting atoms, which are the tiny building blocks for everything on Earth

pedestrian A walking person

profits Financial gains: difference between monies earned and spent

prototype The first model of a design

radar A system that detects objects by sending out radio waves

sabotaged Deliberately damaged

semi-truck A powerful truck with a trailer half supported by its own wheels

sensor A device that detects physical properties, such as heat and sound

smog A fog made worse by pollution

solar-powered Taking energy from the Sun

stealth Able to avoid detection by radar

supercapacitors Devices that can store a large amount of electrical energy

three-dimensional (3-D) Having three dimensions—height, width, and length

toxic Poisonous

trade secrets Secret processes used by companies to make products

truce An agreement to stop fighting for a certain time

viral Spread quickly and widely over the Internet

wirelessly Using signals sent through the air, often as radio waves

LEARNING MORE

BOOKS

Hinote Lanier, Wendy. *Transportation Technology Inspired by Nature* (Inspired by Nature). Focus Readers, 2018.

Lake, Joss. *The Evolution of Transportation Technology* (Evolving Technology). Rosen Education Service, 2018.

Perritano, John. *Transportation* (STEM in Current Events). Mason Crest Publishers, 2016.

Verstraete, Larry. *Innovations in Transportation* (Problem Solved! Your Turn to Think Big!). Crabtree Publishing, 2017.

WEBSITES

https://science.howstuffworks.com/transport/engines-equipment/maglev-train.htm
Do some more research into how maglev trains work.

www.dkfindout.com/uk/transport/history-trains
Find out more about the history of train travel.

www.esa.int/esaKIDSen/SEMVTY6QBIJ_Technology_0.html
Explore the technology behind the hyperloop.

www.livescience.com/50841-future-of-driverless-cars.html
Learn more about self-driving cars and the problems they face.

INDEX

ABOUT THE AUTHOR

Megan Kopp is a freelance writer living in the Rockies. She would love to have a personal taxi drone that would whisk her from home to her favorite hiking trail in record time!